The Outdoor Art Room
Art for
WINTER

Rita Storey

WINDMILL
BOOKS

Published in 2018 by **Windmill Books**, an Imprint of Rosen Publishing
29 East 21ˢᵗ Street, New York, NY 10010

Series editor: Sarah Peutrill
Art direction: Peter Scoulding
Series designed and created for Franklin Watts by Storeybooks
rita@storeybooks.co.uk
Designer: Rita Storey
Editor: Sarah Ridley
Photography: Tudor Photography, Banbury
Cover images: Tudor Photography, Banbury
Cover design: Cathryn Gilbert

Cataloging-in-Publication Data
Names: Storey, Rita.
Title: Art for winter / Rita Storey.
Description: New York : Windmill Books, 2018. | Series: The outdoor art room | Includes index.
Identifiers: ISBN 9781508194699 (pbk.) | ISBN 9781508194200 (library bound) |
ISBN 9781508194736 (6 pack)
Subjects: LCSH: Handicraft--Juvenile literature. | Winter--Juvenile literature.
Classification: LCC TT160.S76 2018 | DDC 745.5--dc23

Manufactured in China
CPSIA Compliance Information: Batch BW18WM: For Further Information contact
Rosen Publishing, New York, New York at 1-800-237-9932

Before you start

Some of the projects in this book require scissors or a sewing needle and the handling of ice and peanuts. When using these things we would recommend that children are supervised by a responsible adult.

Contents

All about winter 4

Snow scene 6

Glow stick lanterns 8

Decorate a tree for the birds . 10

Giant spider 14

Multicolored web 16

Ice bowl 18

Stone art 20

Rainbow ice sculptures 22

Snow animals 24

Giant snowflake 26

Ice suncatchers 28

Winter words 30

Find out more 31

Index 32

All about winter

The cold, frosty days of winter can be a great time to get outside if you put on warm clothes. This book is full of art projects and things to make and do outside in winter. Have fun!

When is winter?

Winter happens at different times of the year in different parts of the world. In the northern half of the world, winter lasts from December until March (or until the temperature rises and we see the signs of spring in nature). In the southern half, it lasts from June to September.

Winter is the season between fall and spring. It has the shortest days and longest nights of all the seasons. As the days grow shorter, the temperature drops and it can be cold and wet. Overnight frosts, sleet, and snow are all possible in winter. In the morning, cars are often covered with white frost. Puddles, ponds, and lakes can turn to ice.

It is important to wear warm clothes when you go outside in winter. Keep away from frozen ponds, but have fun cracking the ice on puddles.

What happens in winter?

There is less food for animals to eat in the winter, so they have to find ways to survive. Some birds fly to warmer countries. Animals that stay have to adapt to the colder temperatures. They do this in many different ways. Some animals prepare for winter by eating as much food as they can before finding a place to sleep until it gets warmer. This is called hibernation. They may find shelter in holes in the ground or under rocks and leaves, or grow extra fur to keep out the cold.

The snow and ice in winter mean that people can take part in winter sports such as skiing and snowboarding. A lot of snow can mean that schools have to close. This is a perfect opportunity to go sledding and make snowmen.

snow scene

W inter brings snow to many parts of the world. Even if you do not have any snow, you can use fake snow to build a snow scene.

1 Tip the baking soda into the bowl. Add a 3-second squirt of shaving foam.

You will need:

* 18 ounces (500 g) of baking soda
* large mixing bowl
* shaving foam
* fork
* plastic tray
* model house (optional)
* 2 red beads
* 3 green beads
* 5 small black beads
* tiny twigs

2 Stir with a fork until the mixture has a snowy texture.

3 Put three-quarters of the mixture into a tray. If you have a model house, place it on the fake snow.

Trees in winter

Many trees are bare in winter. Their leaves fell off during the fall months. Fall and winter storms sometimes make twigs break off the trees and fall to the ground. Collect some to use in art projects.

4 Add another 3-second squirt of shaving foam and mix it into the remaining mixture.

To make the snowman

5 Take half of the remaining fake snow and roll it into three balls. Stack them one on top of the other in the tray. Push the beads and twigs into the balls of snow, as shown in the picture.

To make the reindeer

6 Roll the rest of the fake snow into two balls. Stack one on top of the other. Push the beads and twigs into the balls as shown in the picture on the right.

Good news!
This fake snow does not melt, but it does dry out after a few days.

Glow stick lanterns

Cheer up a dark winter evening with these colorful glow stick lanterns.

You will need:

* clear glass bottles and jars
* squares of blue and red tissue paper
* squares of purple tissue paper
* PVA glue
* paintbrush
* glitter glue
* glow sticks (3 or 4 per bottle or jar)

1 Paint PVA glue onto some blue squares of tissue paper. Stick them around the outside of a bottle so that one corner of each square points upwards.

2 Paint PVA glue onto some red squares. Stick them around the bottle above the blue squares so that one corner of each square points upwards.

3 Repeat step 2 with the purple squares. Stick them above the red squares, as shown. Draw a line of glitter glue around each square. Leave to dry.

4 Follow steps 1–3 to decorate more bottles or jars. You could use different colored paper.

8

5 When it gets dark, bend the glow sticks so that they begin to glow.

6 Share the glow sticks among the jars and bottles.

Be patient. Do not bend the glow sticks until it is completely dark.

Light in winter

In the winter the days are short and the nights are long. The lengths of the days and nights vary from country to country, depending on how far north they are. At the North Pole, there are 11 weeks of complete darkness in midwinter.

9

Decorate a tree for the birds

These pretty bird treats look great on the bare branches of a tree in winter. Watch to see how many different types of bird visit your tree.

1 Pour the bird seed into the mixing bowl. Ask an adult to melt the lard in the saucepan. Leave it to cool for 5 minutes. Stir it into the seeds.

You will need:

* 2 ounces (50 g) bird seed
* medium-sized mixing bowl
* 2 ounces (50 g) lard
* saucepan
* wooden spoon
* star cookie cutter
* aluminum foil
* pieces of raffia 8 inches (20 cm) in length

2 Wrap foil around the bottom and sides of the cookie cutter, as shown.

Birds in winter

Birds have several layers of fluffy feathers to trap heat and keep them warm in cold weather. Finding food can be more of a problem in winter, which is why it is a good idea to feed garden birds.

10

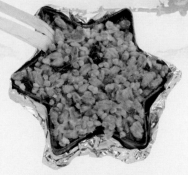

3 Half-fill the star mold with the seed mixture. Fold a piece of raffia in half and place the folded end on the seed mixture.

4 Fill the star mold to the top, covering the end of the raffia as shown.

5 Put the star mold in the freezer. When the mixture is hard, press it out of the mold. Tie the bird feed star onto a tree.

6 Repeat steps 2–5 using a tree-shaped cutter.

Turn the page to find out how to make the other bird decorations on this tree.

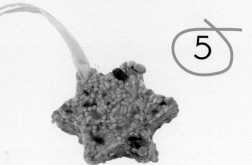

11

These bird treats will attract lots of birds to a bare winter branch. Some birds feed on the ground, so you could put some treats on the ground for them to enjoy as well.

To make the pomegranate decoration

Ask an adult to thread the needle with thin string. Push the needle through the top of each pomegranate slice. Tie the decoration onto a twig. Repeat to make more like this.

You will need:

for the pomegranate decorations

* pomegranate, cut into slices
* embroidery needle
* thin string, cut into 8-inch (20 cm) lengths

for the cereal loops decoration

* cereal loops
* thin string, cut into 12-inch (30 cm) lengths

To make the cereal loops decoration

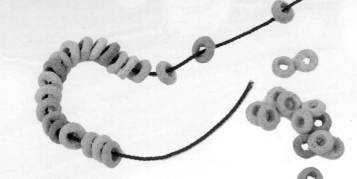

Thread cereal loops onto the string. Tie the ends of the string together. Hang your cereal loop on a twig in a sheltered place to avoid the loops getting soggy. Repeat to make more.

You will need:

for the apple decoration

* an apple, sliced across the middle
* 4 blueberries
* embroidery needle
* thin string, cut into 6-inch (15 cm) lengths

for the popcorn garland

* plain "popped" popcorn
* blueberries
* embroidery needle
* long piece of thread, 20 inches (50 cm) in length

To make the apple and blueberry decoration

Tie a knot in the string. Ask an adult to thread a needle onto the other end and then push it through an apple slice and a blueberry. Repeat to create several layers. Tie the decoration onto a branch.

To make the popcorn garland

Ask an adult to thread the needle with thin string. Push the needle through a piece of plain "popped" popcorn and then through a blueberry. Repeat until your garland is long enough.

Birds need fresh water to drink in winter. Put a shallow bowl of water in your garden. Remember to change it regularly, especially in cold weather.

13

Giant spider

Some garden spiders take shelter in our homes over the winter, while others make webs inside hollow logs or in sheds. This spider is looking for a big meal before he finds a place to spend the winter.

You will need:

* * black or dark purple paint and a paintbrush
* * foam balls, small and large
* * 2 toothpicks
* * 2 googly eyes
* * PVA glue and spreader
* * 4 black pipe cleaners
* * scissors
* * ruler

1 Paint the foam balls black or dark purple.

2 Push a toothpick into one of the foam balls.

3 Push the second foam ball onto the other end of the toothpick until the two balls meet.

(4) Glue on the googly eyes.

(5) Cut the pipe cleaners in half. Bend the ends of each pipe cleaner, as shown above.

(6) Use a toothpick to make four holes in a row on each side of the spider's body.

(7) Push the end of each pipe cleaner into the eight holes in the foam ball.

Turn the page to make a huge web for your spider, so that he can catch a giant fly.

Multicolored web

Spiders spin beautiful webs from silk thread to catch insects. Look outdoors for webs sparkling with frost in early winter.

You will need:

* 1 piece of orange raffia, 6 inches (15 cm) long
* 6 pieces of raffia in different colors, 10 inches (25 cm) long
* 4 long lengths of red, green, pink, and yellow raffia
* scissors

(1) Tie the ends of the length of orange raffia together to make a loop.

(2) Knot the six longer lengths of raffia onto the orange loop.

(3) Tie the ends of each length of raffia onto the branches of a tree, as shown in the photo on the left. Trim the ends.

4 Tie the end of the long length of red raffia onto one of the shorter strings, about 2 inches (5 cm) from the orange loop at the center. Wrap the raffia around the next string, keeping it tight, but not too tight. Wrap it around the next string.

5 Repeat all the way around and tie the end of the raffia in a knot.

6 Repeat steps 4 and 5 with the green, pink, and yellow strings of raffia.

Look who has moved in! It is the giant spider from pages 14–15 trying to catch a fly!

17

Ice bowl

To make this bowl outside, you need very cold weather. As the ice bowl starts to melt, birds can eat the seeds and nuts trapped in the ice.

1

Pour 8 ounces (200 ml) of water into the large bowl. Put the medium-sized bowl inside the large bowl.

You will need:

* 8 ounces (200 ml) of water
* large plastic bowl
* medium-sized bowl
* seeds, berries, leaves, nuts, cereal
* ruler

2

Arrange the seeds, berries, leaves, nuts, and cereal in the space between the two bowls.

All about ice

When water gets very cold, it stops being a liquid and turns into a solid block called ice. To turn water into ice the temperature has to be below 32 °F (0 °C).

18

3 Pour the water between the two bowls until the water level is about 1 inch (3 cm) from the top of the smaller bowl. Put the bowl outside overnight.

4 Pour some warm water into the medium-sized bowl to loosen it. Take it out and place it to one side. Now dip the large bowl in warm water briefly so that you can slide it off your ice bowl.

5 Place the finished ice bowl where the birds will find it outdoors. As the ice melts, it will also create a drinking bowl for the birds.

If the temperature outside is not low enough to turn the water to solid ice, put the bowls into the freezer for two hours.

stone art

In the winter there are very few colorful flowers in the garden. These painted stones will add a splash of color until the flowers bloom again in spring.

1 Paint the stones different colors. Leave to dry.

You will need:

* small, flat stones
* red, orange, yellow, blue, and purple acrylic paint
* paintbrush

2 Paint a spot on each stone in a contrasting color. Leave to dry.

3 Finish by painting a colored dot in the center of each stone. Leave to dry.

4 Lay out your stones on a hard surface. Start in the center, placing the red stones in a spiral shape.

5 Continue with the spiral shape, using the orange stones.

6 Now place the yellow, blue, and purple stones to complete the spiral.

There are lots of other patterns you can make with these colorful stones. Change the pattern every now and again.

Rainbow ice sculptures

Freeze water in an old rubber glove to make an ice sculpture. You could make another shape using a jello mold or a balloon.

You will need:

* old rubber glove (without holes)
* 2 long knitting needles
* ruler
* plastic bucket
* measuring cup
* water
* green, yellow, and blue food coloring
* scissors

This activity will only work when it is VERY cold. If it is not cold enough, use a plastic cup instead of a rubber glove and freeze the sculpture in the freezer.

1 Ask an adult's permission before you use the rubber glove. Ask them to push the knitting needles right through the cuff of the rubber glove, leaving a small gap between the two needles.

2 Balance the knitting needles over the plastic bucket, as shown.

3 Fill the cup with water and add some green food coloring.

4 Fold back the cuff of the rubber glove. Pour the colored water into the glove until the water is up to the top of the fingers. Leave everything outside overnight to freeze hard.

Repeat step 4 with yellow water. Repeat step 4 with blue water.

5 Snip off the glove. Stand the ice hand up somewhere where you can see it as it melts slowly.

Ice hands will begin to melt as soon as the temperature rises above 32 °F (0 °C).

snow animals

If you are lucky enough to have some snow in the winter, why not make a snow caterpillar or a snow bear instead of a snowman?

You will need:

for the caterpillar
* snow * 3 twigs
* 2 seeds

for the snow bear
* snow
* 3 small round stones or pebbles
* 7 small oval stones or pebbles

To make the snow caterpillar

1 Make nine snowballs of the same size.

2 Place the snowballs in a wiggly line.

3 Finish off the caterpillar by adding two twig antennae, two seed eyes and a twig mouth.

Snow

Snowflakes are made when tiny water droplets freeze in the sky to form ice crystals. When enough crystals have joined together, they become heavy and fall as snowflakes.

24

To make the snow bear

1. Make a large snowball and a slightly smaller snowball. Place the smaller one on top.

2. Make seven small snowballs. Place four of them on the bottom snowball to look like arms and legs. Put two on either side of the top snowball to look like ears. Put one onto the middle of the top snowball to look like a muzzle.

3. Use the small round stones to give the bear eyes and a nose. Use the oval stones to add a mouth and three claws on each paw.

Giant snowflake

Flakes of snow are small and delicate, but lots of them can build up in winter to make a thick covering of sparkly snow. This big snowflake will sparkle too as it hangs on a door.

You will need:

* 3 large red popsicle sticks

* strong glue

* 6 small colored popsicle sticks

* PVA glue

* glitter

* 7 sparkly stars

* string

* adhesive tack

If you cannot buy colored popsicle sticks, paint some wooden ones before you begin.

1 Use strong glue to glue two large red popsicle sticks together to form an X.

2 Glue the third red popsicle stick on top to form a six-sided star shape.

3 Glue three small popsicle sticks across the ends of the large sticks, close to the end.

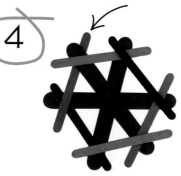

Glue the last small stick under the red popsicle stick

4 Repeat to add three more sticks. Glue the end of the last stick underneath the red popsicle stick, as shown.

5

Spread some PVA glue onto the sticks and sprinkle it with glitter. Shake off the surplus.

6

Glue on a star where the red popsicle sticks cross over each other.

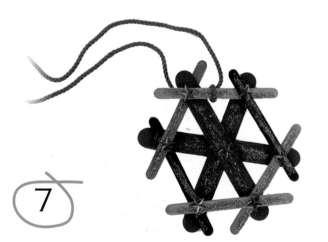

7

Tie the string to the snowflake and knot the ends together to form a loop. Hang the snowflake from a door, using adhesive tack.

snowflakes

Snowflakes all have six points or sides. If you look at a snowflake through a strong magnifying glass you will see a beautiful pattern of ice crystals arranged in a hexagonal pattern. Every snowflake is slightly different.

Ice suncatchers

In very cold weather, it is fun to make ice suncatchers that will sparkle in the winter sunlight.

You will need:

* plastic lid
* water
* sequins
* confetti stars
* glitter
* piece of raffia, 8 inches (20 cm) long
* blue and yellow food coloring

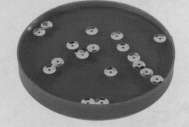

1 Fill the plastic lid with water.

2 Sprinkle a few sequins on top.

3 Add some confetti stars.

4 Sprinkle a little glitter on top.

5 Fold the raffia in half. Lay the folded end in the water. Add one drop of blue food coloring.

6 Put the suncatcher outside overnight. The next morning, dip it in warm water for a few seconds and it will slide out of the plastic lid. Repeat steps 1–6 to make a second ice suncatcher. This time use the yellow food coloring.

Hang the suncatcher outside as soon as you take it out of the lid or put it in the freezer until you are ready to hang it up.

7 Tie the ice suncatchers onto the branch of a tree.

Thawing

To stay frozen, water has to be below freezing. When the temperature is higher than 32 °F (0 °C), the ice suncatchers will slowly melt (turn back to water).

If the temperature outside is not low enough to turn the water to solid ice, put the lids into the freezer for two hours.

Winter words

adapt change or find ways to suit new surroundings

antennae pair of thread-like projections found on the head of insects

droplet tiny drop of water or another liquid

frost frozen dew or water vapor

hexagonal having six sides and six angles

hibernation when animals go into a deep sleep to survive the winter

ice frozen water – its solid state; water freezes when it reaches temperatures below 32 °F (0 °C)

ice crystal a small piece of ice with many even sides

lard pig fat that has been processed for use in cooking

magnifying glass a round piece of glass with a handle that magnifies objects, making them appear bigger than they really are

seed the part of a plant that grows into a new plant

snowflake tiny flake of snow

spider's web a network of fine silk threads that are made inside a spider's body and woven into a web to catch insects

temperature how hot or cold something is

thaw when a substance that was frozen warms up it thaws, becoming softer or liquid

Find out more

For web resources related to the subject of this book, go to: www.windmillbooks.com/weblinks and select this book's title.

Index

birds 5, 10–11, 12–13, 18–19

days 4, 9

fake snow 6–7
food 5, 10–11, 12–13, 18–19
freezing 18, 19, 22–23, 29
frost 4, 16

hibernation 5

ice 4, 5, 18–19, 22–23, 24, 28–29

lanterns 8–9

melting 18, 23, 29

nights 4, 9
North Pole 9

reindeer 7

snow 4, 5, 6–7, 24–25, 26, 27
snowflakes 24, 26–27
snowmen 5, 7, 24
spiders 14–15, 16–17
spring 4, 20

thawing 29
trees 6, 10, 11, 16, 29

webs 14, 15, 16–17